MW01635748

written by Judy Zocchi

illustrated by Rebecca Wallis

dingles&company New Jersey

First printing

PUBLISHED BY dingles&company

P.O. Box 508 • Sea Girt, New Jersey • 08750

WEBSITE: www.dingles.com • E-MAIL: info@dingles.com

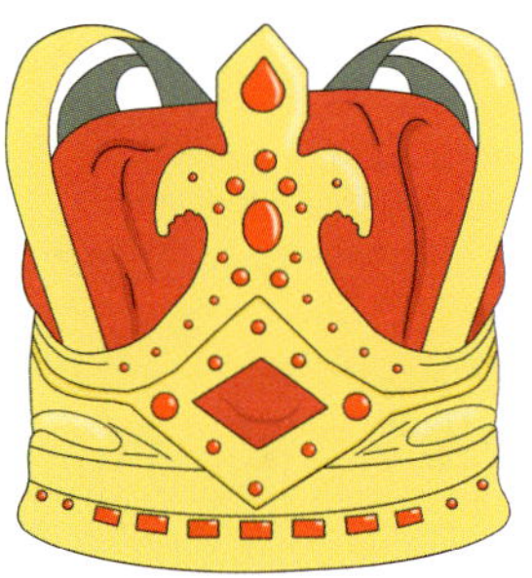

Library of Congress Catalog Card No.: **2004091574**

ISBN: **1-891997-53-X**

Printed in the United States of America

For Fabiana

ART DIRECTION & DESIGN **Barbie Lambert**

EDITED BY **Andrea Curley**

RESEARCH AND ADDITIONAL COPY WRITTEN BY **Robert Neal Kanner**

EDUCATIONAL CONSULTANT **Anita Tarquinio-Marcocci**

DESIGN ASSISTANT **Erin Collity**

CRAFT PHOTOGRAPHY BY **Sara Sagliano**

CRAFT CREATED BY **the Aldorasi family**

PRE-PRESS BY **Pixel Graphics**

Holiday Happenings

examines the
most popular holidays
celebrated by various cultures.
The series explains
the origin of each day
as well as popular traditions
and activities
associated with it.

On Three Kings Day you might wake up early

Children who celebrate this holiday are too excited to sleep late because they know that they probably have presents waiting for them when they awake.

It is a custom for parents to tell their children that if they leave their shoes by their beds, the Three Kings might visit during the night and fill them with small gifts.

to find gifts in the shoes you left by your bed.

Then you make a king's crown to wear on your head.

A popular custom in Hispanic neighborhoods is to have local community leaders dress up as the Three Kings. They then lead a parade to commemorate the Three Kings' journey to find the baby Jesus.

On Three Kings Day you might dress up like a king

Purple is a symbol of royalty because the dye was so rare and expensive that only royalty could afford to buy it.

in a costume made of purple suede.

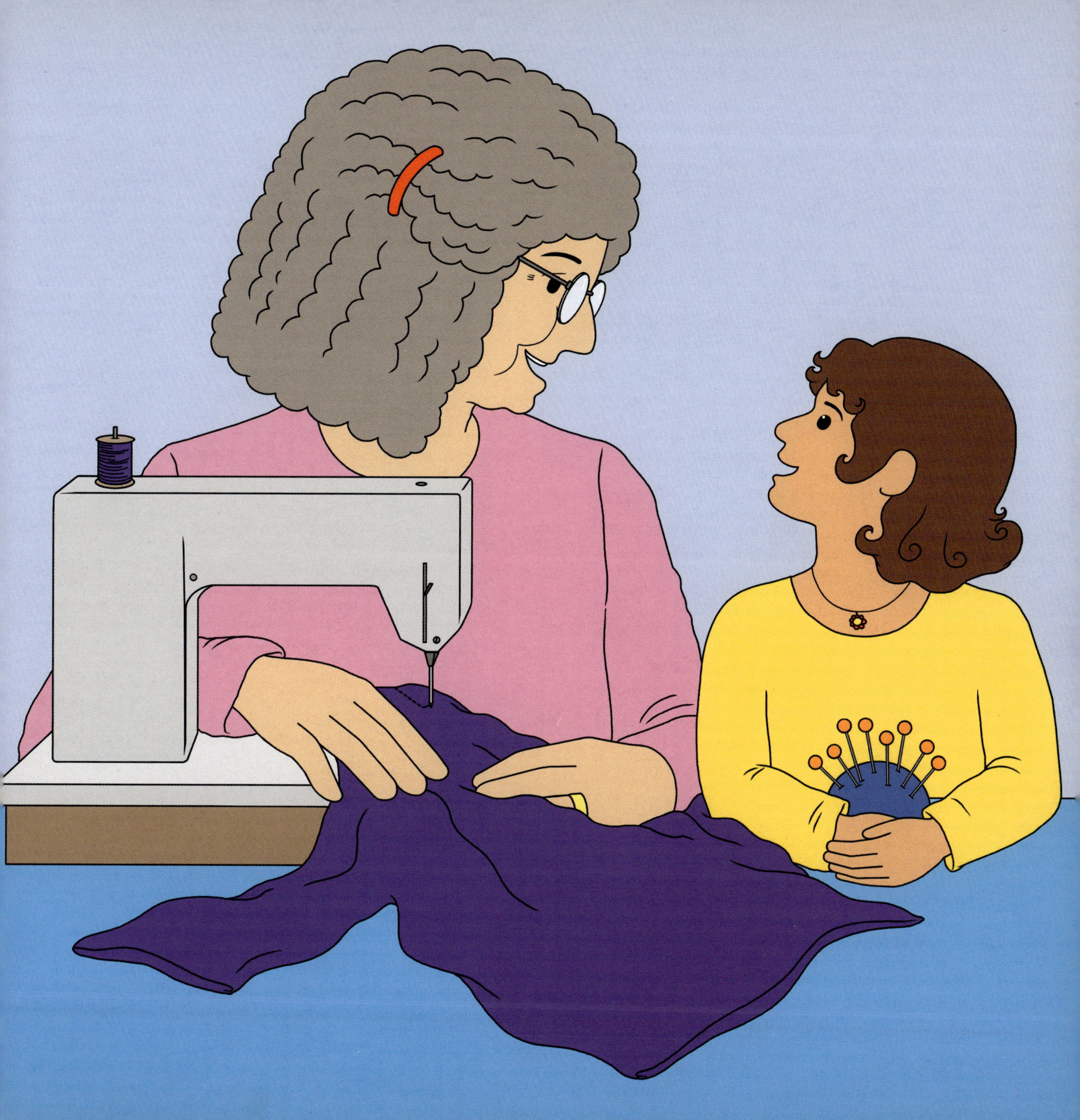

Then you walk next to camels in a city parade.

On Three Kings Day you might help to bake a special cake

A holiday tradition is to bake a cake or sweetbread in the shape of a crown. It is then decorated with candied fruits to resemble jewels.

with a statue of a baby inside.

A popular custom
is to hide a tiny figure of
a baby that represents the baby
Jesus in the cake or bread.

The lucky person who finds it might be right at your side!

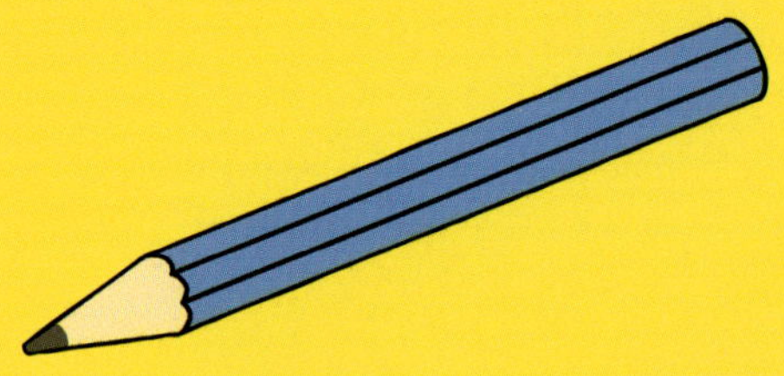

A crown or jeweled headdress symbolizes the Three Kings.

On Three Kings Day you could put your name in a crown

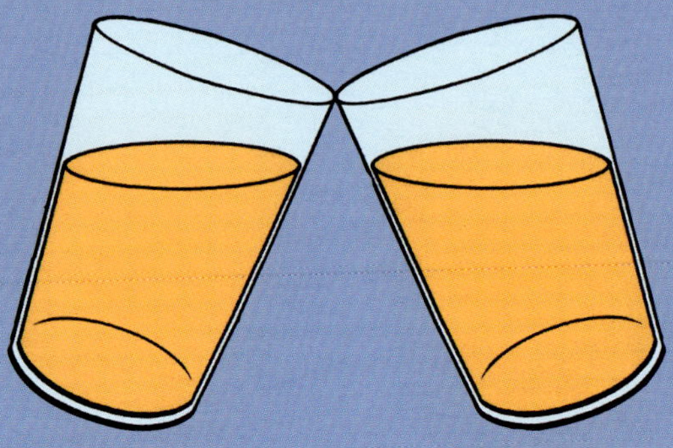

and make a holiday toast.

Sometimes before drinking, a person will raise his or her glass and make a short speech in honor of someone or something.

Then you pick out the name of the next party's host!

MARIA

Three Kings Day

is a Christian holiday. It commemorates the biblical story of the Three Wise Men, also called the Three Kings. They followed a special star to find the newborn baby Jesus and gave him gifts. Christians consider Jesus to be the Son of God. The holiday is celebrated on January 6.

Three Kings Day is widely observed by Hispanics around the world. They often exchange gifts on Three Kings Day rather than on Christmas. Many traditions are followed on this holiday. The evening before Three Kings Day, Hispanic children may leave their shoes near their beds before going to bed, often filling them with hay for the kings' camels. The children hope that the Three Kings will leave them presents. On the holiday itself, many Hispanic communities hold parades with live camels, men dressed as kings, and music. Families also get together for a big meal. For dessert, they eat the Rosca de Reyes. This is a crown-shaped sweetbread decorated with candied fruit. Inside are one or more figurines of the baby Jesus. Whoever finds one of the figurines inside his or her piece of the Rosca is supposed to invite everyone to his or her house for Candelaria. This is the last celebration of the Christmas season and is held forty days after the birth of Jesus.

DID YOU KNOW...

Use the Holiday Happenings series to expose children to the world around them.

- In Puerto Rico, children sometimes cut grass and put it in a shoebox under their beds for the Three Kings' camels to eat. The children's gift wish list for the holiday is placed on top of the grass.
- According to an Italian legend, when the Wise Men were on their way to Bethlehem, they asked a kindly old witch, La Bafana, to go with them to see the baby Jesus. She refused and missed the miracle birth. Now La Bafana flies from house to house on her broom looking for Jesus and leaving presents.
- In the Philippines, people display star lanterns, which symbolizes the star of Bethlehem.
- During the late nineteenth century in France, a loaf of bread was baked with a lima bean inside, and the person who found it in his or her piece would receive a gift from the king. Today, the French bake a cake with a surprise inside of it.

BUILDING CHARACTER...

Use the Holiday Happenings series to help instill positive character traits in your children. This Three Kings Day emphasize dependability.

- Has someone ever depended on you?
- Were you dependable, or did you let him or her down?
- How can you make sure you are dependable and do not let people down?
- Why is it important to be dependable to yourself and to others?

CULTURE CONNECTION...

Use the Holiday Happenings series to expand children's view of other cultures.

- Find out which countries celebrate Three Kings Day.
- How do people in other countries celebrate Three Kings Day?
- Are these celebrations similar to the way people celebrate Three Kings Day in your country?

TRY SOMETHING NEW...

To help yourself be more dependable, make a list of the things you have to do. Next to the items, put the dates by which they have to be completed. Cross things off of the list as you do them.

For more information on the Holiday Happenings series or to find activities that coordinate with it, explore our website at **www.dingles.com**.

Craft

Three Kings Crown

Goal: To make a crown like the ones used to celebrate Three Kings Day.

Craft: A crown

Materials: Construction paper, crayons, markers, glitter, uncooked macaroni (such as elbow, rigatoni, or ziti) aluminum foil, ruler, stapler, and glue

Directions:

1. With your parents' permission, tear 14 inches of aluminum foil from the roll.
2. Center a piece of construction paper on the foil.
3. Cover one side of the construction paper with glue. Flip over the paper so that the glue side is against the foil. Smooth out the paper. Put glue on the edge of the foil that is sticking out past the edge of the paper. Neatly fold the foil over the top of the paper. Do this on the other three sides.
4. Cover another piece of construction paper with aluminum foil in the same way as you did before.
5. Turn the two pieces of foil-covered paper so that their short ends line up with each other. Then overlap the short edges slightly to make one long piece of paper. Glue the overlapped edges together and smooth them down with your finger. Allow the glued edges to dry thoroughly.
6. While you are waiting for the glue to dry, color your "macaroni jewels" with markers.
7. Once the glue on the foil-covered papers has dried, use scissors to cut a zigzag pattern horizontally across the middle of the glued-together papers. This way you can make two crowns if you wish.
8. Glue the colored macaroni across the left piece of the glued-together papers. Next, using glue, trace around the macaroni. Then sprinkle glitter around the "jewels" so it sticks to the glue. Be creative and decorate the crown however you like.
9. Once the glue has dried, have someone help you wrap the crown around your head and mark it to fit the size of your head. Cut off the excess paper and use a stapler or glue to fasten the two sides of the crown where it was marked.
10. Now you are ready to dress up like a king in honor of Three Kings Day!

Judy Zocchi

is the author of the Global Adventures, Holiday Happenings, Click & Squeak's Computer Basics, and Paulie and Sasha series. She is a writer and lyricist who holds a bachelor's degree in fine arts/theater from Mount Saint Mary's College and a master's degree in educational theater from New York University. She lives in Manasquan, New Jersey, with her husband, David.

Rebecca Wallis

was born in Cornwall, England, and has a bachelor's degree in illustration from Falmouth College of Arts. She has illustrated a wide variety of books for children, and she divides her time between Cornwall and London.